Exploring Ancient

ROME

with Elaine Landau

Enslow Elementary

an imprint of

Enslow Publishers, Inc.

40 Industrial Road   PO Box 38
Box 398   Aldershot
Berkeley Heights, NJ 07922   Hants GU12 6BP
USA   UK

http://www.enslow.com

"The 'Exploring Ancient Civilizations With Elaine Landau' series tells the stories of the Egyptians, Greeks, Romans, Chinese, Vikings, and Aztecs with texts and illustrations designed to appeal to a broad spectrum of students. While not refraining from acknowledging injustice, hardship, and even the brutality of pre-modern civilizations, the series nonetheless succeeds in presenting these six ancient peoples in a dignified, praiseworthy, and even exemplary light. Highly recommended."

—Nicholas F. Jones, Professor of Classics, University of Pittsburgh

Library of Congress Cataloging-in-Publication Data

Landau, Elaine.
    Exploring ancient Rome with Elaine Landau / Elaine Landau.— 1st ed.
      p. cm. — (Exploring ancient civilizations with Elaine Landau)
    Includes bibliographical references and index.
    . ISBN 0-7660-2337-0
    1. Rome—Civilization—Juvenile literature. I. Title.
    DG78.L35 2005
    937'.6—dc22

                    2004010987

Printed in the United States of America

10 9 8 7 6 5 4 3 2 1

To Our Readers: We have done our best to make sure all Internet addresses in this book were active and appropriate when we went to press. However, the author and the publisher have no control over and assume no liability for the material available on those Internet sites or on other Web sites they may link to. Any comments or suggestions can be sent by e-mail to comments@enslow.com or to the address on the back cover.

Illustration Credits: © 1999 Artville, L.L.C. All rights reserved., p. 4, Ann Ronan Picture Library/HIP/The Image Works, p. 25 (bottom); Clipart.com, p. 11 (bottom), 13, 14, 18 (top), 22 (top), 31 (bottom), 33 (top), 37 (bottom), 40 (top), 47; CM Dixon/HIP/The Image Works, pp. 15 (top), 29; © Corel Corporation, pp. 2, 5, 6, 9, 10 (bottom) 11 (top), 16, 17 (bottom), 18 (bottom), 20, 21, 22 (bottom), 24, 25 (top), 26, 28, 31 (middle), 32, 33 (bottom), 34 (bottom), 35, and 39, 41 (top), 45, 46; Elaine Landau, p. 42; Enslow Publishers, Inc., pp. 4–5 (map), 7 (top), 30; Illustration by David Pavelonis, pp. 3, 7 (bottom), 10 (top), 12, 15 (bottom), 19, 23 (top), 27, 31 (top), 34 (top), 37 (top), 40 (bottom), 41 (bottom), and on pp. 1, 5, 6, 42; © Hemera Technologies, Inc., pp. 36, 38, and 43–44; Kristin McCarthy, 17 (top), 23 (bottom); © 1995-2001 Nova Development Corporation, p. 14 (bottom); Photos.com, p. 1; Pietro de Cortona, p. 8.

Front Cover Illustrations: David Pavelonis (Elaine & Max drawings); Kristin McCarthy (coins) Photos.com (helmet and Colosseum).

Back Cover Illustrations: © Corel Corporation (pottery); David Pavelonis (Elaine & Max drawings);

Contents

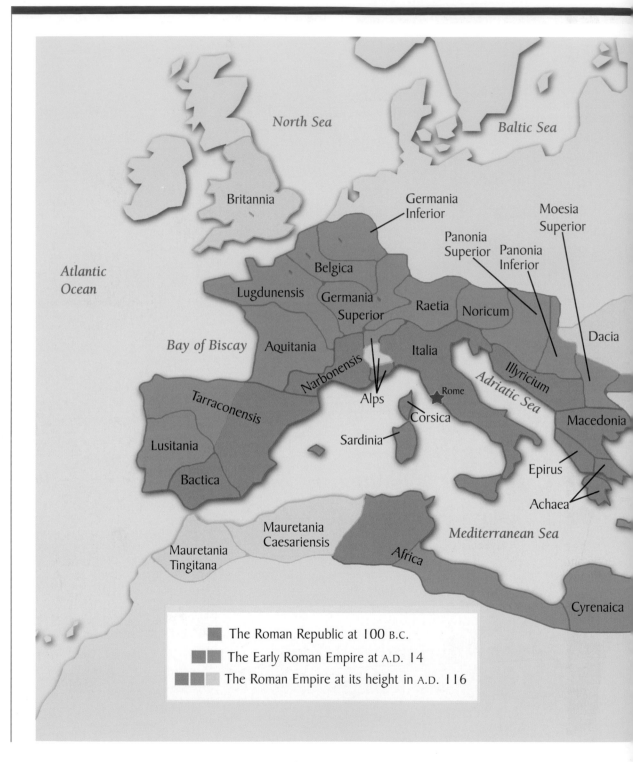

North Sea

Baltic Sea

Britannia

Germania
Inferior

Moesia
Superior

Panonia
Superior   Panonia
Inferior

Atlantic
Ocean

Belgica

Lugdunensis

Germania
Superior

Raetia

Noricum

Dacia

Bay of Biscay

Aquitania

Italia

Illyricum

Adriatic Sea

Narbonensis

Alps

Rome

Tarraconensis

Corsica

Macedonia

Lusitania

Sardinia

Bactica

Epirus

Achaea

Mauretania
Caesariensis

Mediterranean Sea

Mauretania
Tingitana

Africa

Cyrenaica

The Roman Republic at 100 B.C.

The Early Roman Empire at A.D. 14

The Roman Empire at its height in A.D. 116

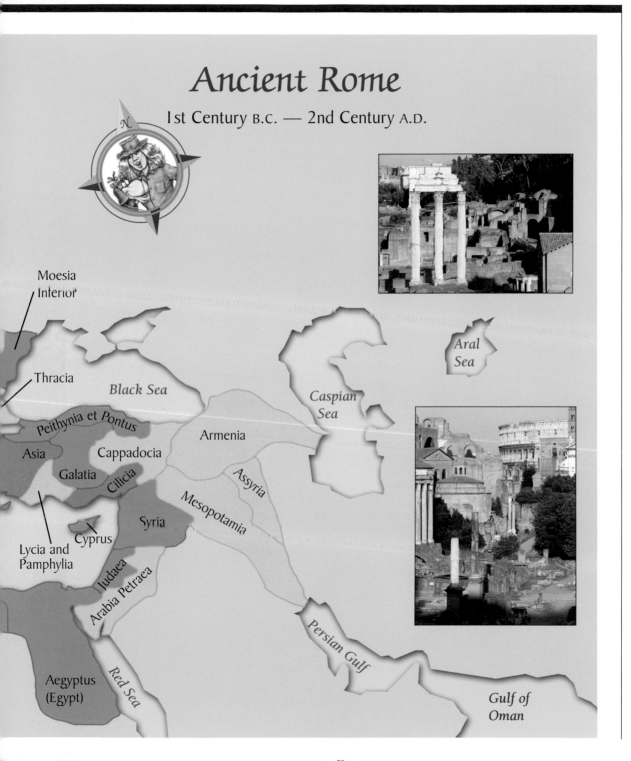

Ancient Rome

1st Century B.C. — 2nd Century A.D.

Moesia
Inferior

Thracia

Black Sea

Peithynia et Pontus

Asia

Galatia

Cappadocia

Cilicia

Lycia and
Pamphylia

Cyprus

Syria

Iudaea

Arabia Petraea

Aegyptus
(Egypt)

Red Sea

Armenia

Assyria

Mesopotamia

Caspian
Sea

Aral
Sea

Persian Gulf

Gulf of
Oman

Dear Fellow Explorer,

What if you could travel back in time? If you could go anywhere in the whole wide world, where would you stop? Perhaps you would like to visit an ancient civilization. How about seeing a nation that was a great military power? The country I have in mind built up a massive empire and over time controlled most of Europe as well as parts of Asia and the northern coast of Africa.

If this sounds like an exciting place to you—set the dial on your time machine to the 2nd century A.D. and head for ancient Rome! You may actually feel somewhat at home there. Many of the things we use today date back to ancient Rome. Our legal system is based on the Roman view of law and justice. They had a jury system just as we do. A number of modern languages are also based on Latin—the language of the ancient Romans. Many English

Check out this picture of the Temple of Antonius and Faustina. This is just one of the many wonders we'll see in Ancient Rome.

1	I	8	VIII
2	II	9	IX
3	III	10	X
4	IV	50	L
5	V	100	C
6	VI	500	D
7	VII	1,000	M

Movie companies often use Roman numerals to show when a movie was released. For example, *Shrek 2*, which was released in 2004, would have the year written as MMIV.

words come from Latin. You may even know someone who is taking Latin in high school.

If you had any math homework this week, you probably used numbers. The ancient Romans influenced our number system too. It is not hard to find a clock with Roman numerals. Ancient Rome's architecture, engineering, and art also affected our culture.

I'm Elaine Landau and this is my dog Max. Max and I are about to take a trip back in time to ancient Rome. The trip was Max's idea. He wanted to know what Rome was like long before he was born. Come along with us. There is a lot to see. Don't worry about the time—with time travel, you can always be back before dinner!

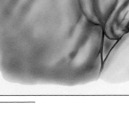

OH MAX. YOU DON'T HAVE TO BARK IN LATIN...BARKING IS A UNIVERSAL LANGUAGE!!

History

There is a legend about how Rome began. It says that Rome was started by twin brothers named Romulus and Remus. They were the sons of Mars, the Roman god of war. In the legend, the twins were thrown into the Tiber River to die. Yet they survived after being washed ashore and raised by a she-wolf.

The boys grew into men and built a city on the spot where they had been thrown into the river. But the brothers quarreled and Remus was killed by his brother. Romulus named the city "Rome" after himself and reigned there as king. That is the legend, but that is not really how Rome started.

The early Romans lived in small villages in the seven hills of Rome. These were near the Tiber River in the country we know today as Italy. These people were farmers and shepherds who lived in simple huts. Over time, the different

The shepard Faustulus found Romulus and Remus with the she-wolf. This painting shows Faustulus taking one of the brothers to his family.

The Tiber River often floods. Walls were built to keep the flood waters out. This picture shows how the Tiber River looks today.

villages united to form one larger city known as Rome. A leader named Romulus became Rome's first king in 753 B.C. Rome continued to be ruled by kings for some time. This was so even after the Romans invaded the Etruscans, a group from the north.

Between 700 and 600 B.C., Rome thrived under the Etruscan kings. Impressive buildings began to be built and trade increased. However, by 509 B.C., the Romans had had their fill of kings. They rebelled and overthrew the last one. Now the Romans set up a republic. In a republic, the leaders are elected.

Yet the republic did not last, either. The government was made up of wealthy men who ignored the needs of

the poor. Soldiers in the army often proved to be more loyal to their generals than to Rome's government.

Julius Caesar was a consul (a type of government leader) who gained great power. He ruled Rome until he was killed by enemies in 44 B.C. Following a series of civil wars, the republic fell. After that, a number of emperors reigned in Rome. Gaius Octavius, who was given the title of Augustus by the Roman Senate, became the first Roman emperor in 27 B.C. He never called himself an emperor though. Instead, he used titles like "first citizen." While he continued to call Rome a republic, he held all the power.

Before Julius Caesar became emperor, he had spent most of his own money holding sports and games for the people. To the right is a statue of Caesar.

Augustus was not only an emperor, but also an author. He gave money to many other Roman writers of the day because he loved literature so much.

A Roman emperor was in complete control. He was in charge of the troops as well as of Rome itself. The emperor was protected and supported by a huge army.

Augustus reigned until his death in A.D. 14. After his reign, Rome would have both good and bad emperors. During the height of Rome's glory, trade and commerce increased. Rome's conquest of foreign lands continued. People looked to Rome with great respect. Few questioned its tremendous power.

After the reign of Augustus, the Romans invaded Britain in A.D. 43.

2 Roman Society

Not everyone was equal in Roman society. Men of great wealth were at the top of the social ladder. Often these men were born into noble families. Below them were well-to-do businesspeople. The commoners were on a still lower level. Some were farmers, while others had shops. The ancient Roman craftspeople were in this class as well.

Men were the heads of the households in ancient Rome. Women and men were not equal partners in marriage. Roman women had few rights. Unless they were wealthy widows or single women, their lives were largely controlled by their fathers or husbands. Women were expected to marry and have children. They could not vote or hold a government office. Yet some women were known to influence their husbands' decisions in business or politics.

A male child was always a welcome addition to a Roman family. Far more Roman boys than girls were educated. Many went to primary (elementary) school while they were young. There they learned reading, writing, and math. The teachers were quite strict.

JUMPIN' JULIUS CAESAR!!... **WHAT'S THAT!?**

EQUAL RIGHTS FOR WOMEN!!

EQUAL RIGHTS FOR DOGS!!

These Roman girls study a lesson. Only wealthy girls were educated.

A child who did not know his lessons or misbehaved might be hit with a cane.

Wealthy boys were usually taught at home by tutors. Some rich girls were taught at home as well. The boys, however, continued their education to become lawyers or politicians. The children of the poor rarely went to school. They did not learn to read or write and began working at an early age.

Slavery was widespread and accepted in ancient Rome. Many slaves were prisoners of war. At times, people captured by pirates were also sold as slaves. A very wealthy Roman might own thousands of slaves. Slaves worked in his businesses, in his fields, and in his home.

Slaves did not always remain in bondage. Some managed to buy their freedom and that of their children. In some cases, former slaves later bought their own slaves.

Slaves were often prisoners from lands the Romans conquered. Even children were used as slaves.

Government and Law

No one was more powerful than the Roman emperor. Under the emperors, Rome had a governing body known as the Senate. There were also two government heads called consuls. This was the form of government Rome had when it was a republic. But now these individuals did what the emperor wanted. They dared not defy him.

People were expected to obey Roman law. Those charged with crimes were tried by a jury. Juries determined if those accused were guilty. The juries of ancient Rome were larger than the ones we have today. There were often over fifty jurors on a case.

The members of the Roman senate debated many important issues in their chamber.

This bronze statue depicts a man caught by the Romans. The prisoner is from Gaul, which is called France today.

Two people found guilty of the same crime might be treated very differently. Penalties for wealthy Romans were less severe than those for the poor. Slaves received the harshest punishments.

People were not sent to prison for long periods in ancient Rome. Often they were fined or had their property taken. Sometimes they were sent into exile and made to leave Rome. Death sentences were handed out as well. People sentenced to die were often crucified.

LET'S GET OUT OF HERE MAX!...I WOULDN'T WANT TO BE FOUND GUILTY OF ANYTHING IN ANCIENT ROME!!

ROMAN COURT

The World of Work

Ancient Rome was an active and growing city. A wide range of goods and services could be found there. This was partly due to Rome's large workforce. It was made up of people with many talents and skills.

In ancient Rome, a man's work was often connected to his wealth and social class. The men in Rome's Senate were not paid. Senators were already wealthy and served out of a sense of duty to the empire.

Soldiers, on the other hand, were paid. Often men

A soldier's life was very hard. On this Roman column, soldiers are building walls, rowing boats, and battling invading forces.

joined the Roman army to earn a better salary than they might at other jobs. Yet being a soldier was not easy. These men put in long hours and regularly risked their lives fighting for the emperor. At times, they had to march for days before fighting a battle.

Many middle-class Romans were traders. They sold goods from Rome to distant lands as well as brought various products to Rome. Among the items traded were jewelry, furniture, spices, perfumes, and different foods.

Some of the products sold by traders were made by Etruscan or Roman craftsmen. These artisans often had work areas attached to their shops. They fashioned bronze jugs and vases. Glass and pottery items were made. The gold jewelry created by talented goldsmiths was highly

These Roman coins have survived for about two thousand years.

This Etruscan pottery shows Etruscan soldiers and chariot riders. Each chariot had two wheels and was pulled by horses.

The shops of merchants and craftsmen lined many of the streets in ancient Rome.

Victorious Roman soldiers would return to the city of Rome's Forum (above) from distant lands to display the treasure they captured.

prized by wealthy Romans. Silver and copper pieces were also made. Some jewelry was decorated with precious stones.

Blacksmiths were among the busiest craftsmen in ancient Rome. They made useful items such as tools and locks. Blacksmiths also made quite a few kitchen and farm utensils.

At times, slaves ran stores and shops for their wealthy masters. Frequently these shops sold grocery and bakery items. The Forum was a vast trade center in Rome where nearly every type of shop could be found. Romans could buy just about whatever they wanted there.

Some work required backbreaking labor and long hours. This was usually done by slaves. They planted and harvested wheat, millet, barley, olives, and other crops on their master's land. They also tended the fruit tree orchards owned by the rich. However, some skilled slaves were not laborers and were found in many other areas of Rome's world of work.

5 Engineering

*T*he Romans achieved some great engineering feats. You may have heard the expression "All roads lead to Rome." In some ways, this was true. Early on, the Romans realized that roads were important for transportation, trade, and empire building. Roads were especially vital for Rome's military. A region could not be conquered or controlled if soldiers could not get there.

This Roman road is in Algeria, Africa. Despite the saying "all roads lead to Rome," most Romans traveled to the African part of the empire by ship.

This Roman-built aqueduct still stands in Portugal. Water flowed through the channel. An aqueduct carries water over long distances to land that does not get a lot of water naturally.

The ancient Romans engineered an impressive highway system. These roads linked roads to the outlying regions. A person could enter or leave Rome from just about any direction. The Romans built far-reaching road systems throughout their empire as well.

Roman roads were very well made. Each was four layers thick. The Romans invented greatly improved concrete in the 2nd century A.D. and this helped to make both their roads and buildings sturdy.

Bridges were another example of good engineering in ancient Rome. The Romans wedged large stones together to form curved or arch-shaped bridges. These bridges were built in Rome as well as in many parts of their

Roman soldiers sometimes had to build bridges to get to lands they wanted to conquer.

empire. They were so well constructed that some are still standing today.

The arch design was also seen in Rome's famous aqueducts. These were structures built to bring water directly to Rome from outside the city. Water flowing downward through big pipes from surrounding hillsides crossed over valleys on these huge stone arches. All the water flowed into tanks and was distributed throughout the city.

This water supplied Rome's many fountains. Most Romans relied on these fountains for water for cooking, drinking, and washing. Water from Rome's aqueducts was also used for the city's hundreds of public bath houses. Many Romans went to

The Arch of Titus is a good example of a well-built Roman arch.

the baths every day before dinner. These baths were more than just a place to get clean. They also had saunas, libraries, beautiful gardens, and snack areas. People at the baths might have a massage. Some enjoyed meeting their friends there. The Roman baths were extremely popular and often crowded.

Some Roman baths held three thousand people! These are the remains of a Roman bath in England.

Architecture

The ancient Romans were outstanding architects. Any visitor to Rome would be impressed by its buildings. These included the city's spectacular amphitheaters. Amphitheaters were impressive stadium-like structures that were about four stories high. They had a large open space in the center known as the arena. Tiers of seats surrounded the arena. The most famous Roman amphitheater was opened in A.D. 80. It was called the Colosseum and could seat fifty thousand people.

The Roman Colosseum still stands today. The amphitheater could be flooded to stage naval battles.

Amphitheaters were found throughout the Roman empire, including this one in Turkey (left).

Gladiators salute the emperor before their contest. Bodies from the last contest are still on the ground (right).

A great deal of bloodshed went on in the amphitheaters. Here professional fighters called gladiators fought to the death. Sometimes wild animals were brought in to fight each other. In some cases the gladiators fought the animals. Other times, unarmed slaves or prisoners condemned to death were made to face the animals in the arena.

Another famous Roman structure, completed in A.D. 126, was the Pantheon. It was built to honor the gods. The Pantheon had a circular interior and a domed roof. It was decorated with colorful slabs of marble. The

"Pantheon" means "a place for all gods." The Pantheon (left) became a Catholic church after the Roman Empire fell.

The ruins of a Roman Basilica in Pompeii (below). The basilica is where leaders met and criminals were punished.

Pantheon is considered more than a building—it is a work of art.

Basilicas were also fine examples of Roman architecture. These spacious rectangular buildings were sometimes divided by columns. Basilicas were used as courts of law and for some government ceremonies and events. On the outside of these buildings were porticos, which were like open porches. The porticos were covered by roofs supported by columns. Traders frequently used these spaces to sell their wares.

Great architecture enhanced the lives of the Romans. In some cases, it was present at their deaths as well. Wealthy Romans had magnificent tombs built for themselves. Some were large, circular, and wonderfully decorated.

CAN YOU IMAGINE BEING BURIED HERE? I DON'T KNOW ANYONE WHO EVEN **LIVES IN A PLACE THIS GRAND!**

Religion

*T*he ancient Romans worshiped many gods and goddesses. There was a different god for nearly every purpose. Jupiter was the king of the gods while Mars was the god of war. Venus was the goddess of love. Mercury was the god who protected trade, and Neptune was the god of the sea. The Romans also believed that their emperors became gods after they died.

There were many magnificent temples in ancient Rome. These were cared for by Roman priests and priestesses. The priestesses were called Vestal Virgins. They were selected for this role as children and were not allowed to marry. The priestesses and priests took part in

Neptune, god of the sea, was often shown carrying a trident. A trident is a spear with three sharp points, which was usually used for fishing.

This picture, showing Romans sacrificing an ox, is in the Temple of Vespasian in Pompeii, Italy.

sacrifices or offerings made to the gods. Bulls, rams, and boars were among the animals sacrificed to please the Roman gods. Coins, jewelry, and costly statues were left as offerings to the gods too.

The Romans also believed in prophets. These were people who claimed to be able to foresee or tell the future. Sometimes prophets did so by looking at lightning during a thunderstorm or watching the patterns of birds in flight.

The Romans allowed people they conquered to go on worshiping their own gods. The same was true for newcomers to Rome. Sometimes the Romans even began to worship the gods of others as well as their own.

However, people of other religions were still required to worship the important Roman gods. Not every group would agree to this. The Jews refused to put statues of Roman gods in their synagogues. The Christians rejected the Roman gods as well. This was because Jews and

Gods and Goddesses

The Romans worshipped many gods and goddesses. Each god or goddess oversaw a part of Roman life.

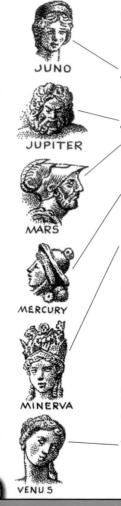

JUNO

JUPITER

MARS

MERCURY

MINERVA

VENUS

Cupid—God of love; Venus's son.

Flora—Goddess of flowers and spring.

Juno—Queen of the gods; goddess of marriage and birth; wife to Jupiter.

Jupiter—King of the gods.

Mars—God of war; son of Jupiter and Juno.

Mercury—God of roads and travel; messenger of the gods; son of Jupiter.

Minerva—Goddess of wisdom; daughter of Jupiter.

Neptune—God of the sea; Jupiter's brother.

Saturn—God of fertility and planting; father of Jupiter and Neptune.

Sol—God of the sun.

Terra—Goddess of the earth.

Venus—Goddess of love and beauty; Cupid's mother.

Christians were not supposed to worship any god except their own.

The Romans were very cruel to the Christians. Many of them suffered and died at the hands of Roman soldiers. Yet in time the situation changed. Years later, other emperors accepted Christianity. In A.D. 313, Christianity was even made the Roman empire's official religion.

The Roman emperor Constantine (right and below) made Christianity the official Roman religion.

Housing

Housing differed sharply according to income level and social class in ancient Rome. Poor people lived in crowded apartment buildings on narrow streets. These all-wood buildings were several stories high and often caught on fire. When this happened the fires quickly spread because the buildings were so close together. These apartment dwellings were dangerous for another reason. Many were so poorly constructed, they sometimes just collapsed.

The homes of the wealthy, on the other hand, were often quite spacious and luxurious. Usually a number of rooms in these homes surrounded an open area called an atrium. Often people enjoyed sitting out in the atrium on warm evenings. Many of these fancy homes had murals (scenes) painted on the walls. The

Homes of the rich usually had big, fancy paintings, known as frescoes, on the walls.

Romans in Pompeii are entertained in their home by a traveling musician playing a lyre.

This foundation of an oval-shaped house still stands today.

HERE WE ARE AT A ROMAN COUNTRY ESTATE. DO YOU WANT TO WALK THROUGH THE ORCHARD OR SPEND SOME TIME IN THE GARDEN **FIRST?**

floors had colorful tile designs on them.

Some wealthy Roman families had both a house in the city and a country estate. Most estates had large beautiful villas on them. The grounds around the villas were attractively landscaped with gardens and

Emperor Hadrian's country villa covered seven square miles. This is the Maritime Theater at Hadrian's villa. The theater was actually used as a place to eat. It was surrounded by water and one had to cross a drawbridge to get to it.

This Roman garden has statues as well as many types of plants.

pools. During the hot summer months, Romans liked to take their children to the countryside. It was cooler there, and there was more space for them to play.

Slaves living in the homes of their wealthy masters did not always enjoy their surroundings. Sometimes they slept in dingy slave quarters in the basement. In other cases, slaves had to find a corner somewhere in the house to sleep.

Food

Wealthy Romans enjoyed food and feasting. They gave lavish dinner parties—offering their guests all sorts of tasty treats. In ancient Rome, cooking was almost considered an art.

The Romans used imported herbs and spices to flavor their food. Romans enjoyed seafood dishes, roasted and stewed meats, and eggs. Pork was among the most popular meats and was often in great demand.

Fruit was usually served at the end of a meal. Romans enjoyed fruits from their own orchards as well as ones imported from other lands. Apples, cherries, pears, plums, figs, and stuffed dates were well-liked choices. These might be eaten with walnuts and almonds or honey cakes. Often fruit was brought out in large glass bowls and people chose what they wanted.

The ancient Romans also tended to drink a great deal of wine. They grew their own grapes and produced different kinds of wines.

Romans enjoyed fruit with their meals.

Today we usually chill wine, but it was served differently in ancient Rome. There it was heated and drunk warm with spices.

Wealthy Romans generally did not eat at a dinner table. Instead they dined while lying down on couches. When entertaining guests, the hosts would have their servants place the food on a

ANOTHER STUFFED DATE...MY DEAR?

At this feast, rich Romans eat while sitting on long couches. The ceiling of this room is painted like the night sky.

low table where it could be easily reached. The couches surrounded the table on three sides.

Bread was an important food staple in ancient Rome. Early on, all bread was home baked. However, as time passed, various breads and other baked goods were sold in bakeries. Well-off Romans preferred white bread made from white flour. The poor of ancient Rome could not afford fancy bread. They usually ate darker bran bread that cost less. Bread and cheese was a common meal for them. They might also have a hunk of bread with a bowl of gruel. Gruel was a watery dish made by boiling a coarsely ground grain in water.

The Romans ate many different kinds of bread. Romans with less money ate darker breads than rich Romans. This was because darker bread was cheaper.

Clothing

C lothing in ancient Rome tended to be loose fitting and comfortable. On most days men wore tunics, which were roomy knee-length garments gathered at the waist. Some tunics had sleeves while others were sleeveless. Perhaps the best-known piece of clothing worn by ancient Romans was the toga. This loose garment was wrapped around a person's body and draped over the left shoulder.

The most common outfit seen on Roman women was a long pleated stola, or tunica, worn over a tunic. The stola was belted at the waist. It was worn indoors, and only by a married woman. For outerwear, women had long cloaks called pallas. These cloaks, which were

These women wear togas. Early on, both men and women wore togas. Later in history, Roman women wore pallas, instead of togas, over their stolas.

often bright red, yellow, or blue, could be draped over the shoulders or pulled up to cover the woman's head. They were worn over the long stolas.

Beauty was important to Roman women. They wore eye makeup, rouge, and lip color to look their best. Some had hairstyles with fancy coiled braids or clusters of curls. Sometimes hairpieces were added to make a woman's hair appear longer or fuller. Decorative blond wigs were popular among rich Roman women too.

Jewelry was another desired item among the wealthy. Rich women had all different kinds of rings, bracelets, pendants, pins, and ankle bracelets. Some even had solid gold hair ornaments set with costly gems. Perfume was also extremely popular in ancient Rome. People paid high prices for special scents imported from the east of the empire.

This Roman woman relaxes while wearing her palla. She has chosen to have it cover her head.

YES. THAT'S THE ONE... IT'S YOU!

The Road Out of Rome

11

Ancient Rome was a great civilization in many ways. Ancient Roman artisans crafted beautiful vases, sculptures, and jewelry. Their architects and engineers built outstanding aqueducts, highways, and buildings. Today these are thought to be priceless reminders of the empire.

Seeing all that ancient Rome had to offer was great. But now it is time for Max and I to leave the wonders of this ancient world. We are glad you came with us on this adventure. Time travel is always more fun with friends. To the time machine!

Rome is still a beautiful city today. Tourists can enjoy the fountain in front of St. Peter's Basilica.

Farewell Fellow Explorer,

I just wanted to tell you about the real "Max and me." I am a children's book author and Max is a small, fluffy, white dog. I almost named him Marshmallow because of how he looks. However, he seems to think he's human—so only a more dignified name would do!

Max also seems to think that he is a large, powerful dog. He fearlessly chases after much larger dogs in the neighborhood. Max was thrilled when the artist for this book drew him as a dog several times his size. He felt that someone in the art world had finally captured his true spirit.

In real life, Max is quite a traveler. I have taken him to nearly every state while doing research for different books. We live in Florida, so when we go north I have to pack a sweater for him. When we were in Oregon it rained, and I was glad I brought his raincoat. None of this gear is necessary for time traveling. My "take off" spot is the computer station, and as always Max sits faithfully by my side.

Best Wishes,
Elaine & Max (a small dog with big dreams)

Timeline

753 B.C.	Rome has its first king.
700–600 B.C.	Rome grows larger and wealthier under the Etruscan kings.
509 B.C.	The Romans rebel and overthrow their last king.
27 B.C.	Augustus becomes the first Roman emperor.
A.D. 14	Augustus dies.
A.D. 80	The Colosseum opens.
A.D. 125	The Pantheon building is completed.
A.D. 200	The Roman Empire is at its height; the Romans improve concrete and building reaches new greatness.
A.D. 313	Christianity becomes the official religion of Rome.
A.D. 476	The Roman Empire falls due to corruption, civil war, and wars in other regions. Its influence is still felt today.

Glossary

amphitheater—A large stadium-like structure with rows of seats in tiers.

aqueducts—Large arch-shaped structures built to carry water directly to Rome from an outside source.

architect—A person who designs buildings.

arena—A large open space used for sports and entertainment.

artisan—A skilled craftsperson.

atrium—The central courtyard area in ancient Roman houses.

basilica—A rectangular building in ancient Rome used as a court of law and for various government ceremonies.

crucified—To be put to death by being nailed to a cross.

defy—To refuse to obey.

empire—A group of countries or regions under the same ruler, who is called an emperor or empress.

feat—A great achievement.

gladiator—A professional warrior who fights others like himself or battles wild animals for the public's entertainment.

irrigation—To supply water to an area by artificial means.

millet—A grass-like grain.

numeral—A written symbol that stands for a number.

palla—A long, brightly-colored wrap of fabric worn by Roman women.

portico—An open porch-like area covered by a roof.

republic—A form of government in which the leaders are elected, instead of being appointed.

sacrifice—An offering made to please the gods.

sauna—A steam bath.

scholar—A person who has a great deal of knowledge.

stola—A long pleated gown belted at the waist.

toga—A loose garment wrapped around the body and draped over the left shoulder.

villa—A large luxurious house in the countryside.

Further Reading

Biesty, Stephen. *Rome: In Spectacular Cross-Section*. Oxford, Eng.: Scholastic Nonfiction, 2003.

Jay, David. *Ancient Romans*. Brookfield, Conn.: Copper Beech Books, 2000.

MacDonald, Fiona. *Ancient Rome*. New York: Kingfisher, 2002.

Raatma, Lucia. *Ancient Rome*. Minneapolis, Minn.: Compass Point Books, 2003.

Williams, Brian. *Ancient Roman War and Weapons*. Chicago: Heinemann Library, 2003.

Wroble, Lisa. *Kids in Ancient Rome*. New York: PowerKids Press, 1999.

Internet Addresses

Ancient Rome

Explore all areas of Roman life.

    <http://www.historyforkids.org>

Under "By Region," click on "Rome."

The Colosseum

See pictures of the remains of Rome's famous Colosseum

    <http://harpy.uccs.edu/>

Under "Image Collections," click "Roman." Click on the "Architecture" link, the select "Colosseum."

Roman-Empire.net

Vote for the best and worst emperor and explore the contests of the gladiators on this fun-filled site.

    <http://www.roman-empire.net/>

Click on "Kids' Section."

Index